THE
LITTLE
CHOCOLATE
BOOK

Jennie Reekie

PIATKUS

Other titles in this series include:

The Little Green Avocado Book
The Little Garlic Book
The Little Pepper Book
The Little Lemon Book
The Little Strawberry Book
The Little Mushroom Book
The Little Bean Book
The Little Rice Book
The Little Tea Book
The Little Coffee Book
The Little Curry Book
The Little Mediterranean Food Book

© 1986 Judy Piatkus (Publishers) Limited

British Library Cataloguing in Publication Data
Reekie, Jennie
    The little chocolate book
    1. Cookery (Chocolate)
    I. Title
    641.6'374   TX767.C5

    ISBN 0-86188-543-0

Drawings by Linda Broad
Designed by Ken Leeder
Cover illustrated by Lynne Robinson

Phototypeset in 10/11pt Linotron Plantin by
Phoenix Photosetting, Chatham
Printed and bound in Great Britain by
The Bath Press, Avon

CONTENTS

The History Of Chocolate   1
Developments In Chocolate Manufacture   7
Chocolate Folklore And Ritual   11
Chocolate Legends   13
Chocolate As An Aphrodisiac   14
Is Chocolate Good For You?   15
Cocoa Butter In Medicine And Cosmetics   19
Facts And Figures   20
From Cacao Beans To Chocolate   21
Making Chocolates   25
Easter Eggs   28
Using Chocolate For Cooking   31
Melting Chocolate   33
Chocolate Petit Fours   35
Chocolate Decorations   36
Chocolate Drinks   37
Chocolate Recipes   41
Acknowledgements   60

'Nature has nowhere else concentrated such an abundance of the most valuable foods in such limited space as in the cocoa bean.'

Alexander von Humboldt, 1796–1859

THE HISTORY OF CHOCOLATE

T he cacao tree (*Theobroma cacao*) is thought to have originated in the Amazon basin and to have been taken to the Yucatan by Mayans in about AD 600. It was highly prized by both the Mayans and the Aztecs, with the beans being used not only to make a drink but as a form of currency.

Cacao played an important part in Aztec mythology. The feathered serpent god, Quetzacoatl, who was reputed to have brought the cacao seeds to Mexico from the Garden of Life, was tricked by a rival god into drinking a potion which destroyed his godly powers. Having buried all his treasures, he disappeared, promising his followers that he would return. When the Spaniard, Hernando Cortés (1485–1547), arrived on the shores of Mexico in 1519, he was initially thought to be the reincarnation of Quetzacoatl. He was immediately received by the Emperor Montezuma (1466–1520), who kept a most sumptuous court.

A detailed description of the banquet given in the Spaniard's honour was later recorded by Bernal Diaz del Castillo, one of the soldiers who accompanied Cortés. According to him, although most of the banquet was served on red and black Cholula ware, the cups for the cacao were made from pure gold. During the course of the meal he says, 'I saw them bring in a good fifty large jugs of this chocolate, all frothed up, of which he [the Emperor] would drink a little.' Following the banquet, all the servants of the court were allowed to eat, and Diaz estimated that at least a thousand plates of food were served and two thousand jugs of frothing chocolate!

Cortés did not repay his host's hospitality with kindness, though. He proceeded to conquer Mexico and kill many of the Aztecs, including Montezuma himself. However, he certainly appreciated the restorative qualities of cacao and on his return to Spain he took some of the beans with him. These were not, in fact, the first cacao beans to be carried back to Spain as it is almost certain that Christopher Columbus, when he landed in Nicaragua 16 years earlier, would have taken some of the beans back home with him. King Ferdinand of Spain, however, had shown little interest in them.

This was possibly because they did not know exactly how to prepare them, and initially 'chocolatl', as it was called by the Mexicans, was not very popular in Spain. Prepared in the Mexican fashion with the roasted bean ground up and mixed with quantities of chilli powder, it is unlikely that it was a very palatable drink. However, the arrival of cacao beans coincided with the discovery of sugar and vanilla, both of which were added to it, rendering it a great deal more pleasant.

For the next century the Spanish jealously guarded their monopoly of cacao and the chocolate trade, but in 1606 this was broken by Antonio Carletti who took the secret of preparing it back to Italy. Jewish exiles and monks carried the recipe to France, and its popularity there increased when the Spanish Princess, Anne of Austria, who was passionate about chocolate and had her own chocolate-making maid, married Louis XIII of France.

In the 16th and 17th century cacao beans were the chief form of currency in Central America. As a result, it was only the rich who could afford to drink 'chocolatl', because for ordinary people it was a case of drinking their money. A rabbit, and a woman for the night cost 10 beans, whilst a 'tolerably good' slave appears to have been a bargain at 100 beans. One Englishman found much to recommend beans as currency, saying, 'Blessed money, which exempts its possessors from avarice, since it cannot be hoarded or hidden underground.'

The first time chocolate appears to have been mentioned in London was in 1657 when a notice appeared in the *Public Advertiser* announcing, 'In Bishopgate St, in Queen's Head Alley at a Frenchman's house, is an excellent West India drink called

Chocolate to be sold, where you may have it ready at any time, and also unmade at reasonable rates.' The 'rate' was between 10–15 shillings a pound, which severely limited the number of people who could afford it.

From the start, heavy excise duty had to be paid on the beans. By the end of the 18th century a duty of 5s10d per pound was due on any beans imported from a country that was not a British possession and it was not until 1853 that this duty was reduced to 2d a pound on the manufactured article and 1d a pound on the raw material which, for the first time, together with new methods of manufacture, made chocolate available to the general public.

CHOCOLATE AND THE CHURCH

Chocolate was accepted almost immediately by the Church, the main controversy about it being an academic one. Was it food, in which case it should be banned during Lent, or a drink, which could be allowed. In 1569 Pope Pius V was given some to try, but he found it so disgusting that he could not imagine anyone ever wanting to drink it, whatever the time of year.

For the next two centuries the debate continued, with countless learned writings by theolgians on the subject. What concerned many was that if chocolate was permitted ways would be found to circumventing fasting with other food, one writer giving as a comparison, 'He who eats 4oz of exquisite sturgeon roasted has broken his fast, if he has it dissolved and prepared in an extract of thick broth he does not sin.'

There was, however, one cleric who developed a violent objection to chocolate – the Bishop of Chiapa. It was not the drink itself to which he took exception, but that the Donnas of Chiapa in Mexico, during a long High Mass insisted on having their serving maids bring them cups of chocolate to sustain them.

The confusion and interruption caused by the serving maids coming in and out of the cathedral with cups of chocolate for their mistresses so distracted the Bishop that he forbade the practice and threatened to excommunicate any who did not obey his order. The ladies, though, paid no heed whatever to this directive and when the priests tried to prevent the maids from delivering the chocolate there was 'uproar' in the cathedral and swords were drawn against the priests. Seeing that he had been defeated, the Bishop resigned his position.

Not long after his resignation, according to Thomas Gage in his *New Survey of the West Indies*, published in 1648, 'The Bishop fell dangerously sick. Physicians were sent for far and neere who all with a joynt opinion agreed that the Bishop was poisoned. A gentlewoman, with whom I was well acquainted, was commonly censured to have prescribed such a cup of chocolate to be ministered by the Page, which poisoned him who so rigorously had forbidden chocolate to be drunk in the church. . . . And it became afterwards a Proverbe in that country: "Beware of the chocolatte of Chiapa".'

COCOA HOUSES

Once Antonio Carletti had taken the recipe for making chocolate back to Italy, it was not long before the famed coffee houses of Venice and Florence became as well known for their chocolate as they were for their coffee.

In England the coffee houses also started serving chocolate, but two houses in London opened specifically for the sale of the new beverage – White's Cocoa House, adjoining St James's Palace, and the Cocoa Tree. Initially White's was known as a somewhat evil gambling den, but later became the first respectable gentleman's club.

The Cocoa Tree at No 64, St James Street was extremely popular during the reign of Queen Anne. It was a haven for Tories, and Defoe in his *Journey Through England* wrote, 'A Whig will no more go to the Cocoa Tree . . . than a Tory will be seen at the coffee house of St James.' Like Whites it also became a gaming house and club, numbering Lord Byron and Gibbon amongst its members.

DEVELOPMENTS IN CHOCOLATE MANUFACTURE

For the first three centuries that chocolate was drunk in the Old World it was a thick, pungent, rather oily drink. 50 per cent of the cacao bean is fat and although some of the fat rose to the surface and could be spooned off, the majority of it remained. In order to counteract this, various farinaceous substances, such as flour, oatmeal, arrowroot and even ground acorns and Irish moss lichen were added to it. Despite the fact that adulteration of cocoa had been banned by an Act passed during the reign of George III, these practices were continued well into the middle and late 19th century, simply because they rendered the drink more palatable.

Undoubtedly the most important turning point in the history of chocolate came in 1828 when Coenraad J. Van Houten developed a hydraulic press which could remove up to two-thirds of the cocoa butter, leaving behind a solid, cake-like substance, cocoa powder, or cocoa essence as it was then called. He also found that the acid in the cocoa could be neutralised, rendering the cocoa more digestible, by adding potash; a process which is still carried on today and is known as 'dutching' in the trade.

Although John Cadbury had made what he called a 'French Eating Chocolate' in 1842, it was only made from roasted beans ground down and mixed with sugar and vanilla, and similar chocolate bars were being produced all over Europe at this time. It was Van Houten's success with his press, designed for making cocoa, which paved the way for Joseph Fry to experiment with the new by-product – cocoa butter. Twenty years after Van Houten's invention, Fry produced the first, high quality chocolate bar by blending the ground cocoa beans with sugar and additional cocoa butter.

Initially all the chocolate produced was plain chocolate, but in 1875 Henri Nestlé, a chemist, was researching into alternative foods for babies who were allergic to mother's milk. A by-product of his research was condensed milk, and this came to the attention of a Swiss chocolatier, Daniel Pieter, who employed Nestlé to experiment with making milk chocolate. Today, production of milk chocolate far outweighs that of plain.

Only five years later a fellow countryman, Rodolphe Lindt, made another important contribution with his discovery of 'conching'. He found that by leaving the chocolate for several days, during which time it was gently stirred and agitated, much of the bitterness and grittiness of the chocolate was removed. It was called 'conching' because the original vat in which he carried out the process was shaped like a conch shell. Conching is still one of the most important processes in the manufacture of chocolate, and in 1899 the firm of Sprüngli from Zurich, considered Lindt's equipment so valuable that they paid 1.5 million gold francs for his factory in Berne and set up the world famous company of Sprüngli and Lindt.

CHOCOLATE PHILANTHROPISTS

Many of the early chocolate manufacturers throughout the world are renowned for their philanthropy and care for their workers. In England this was largely because the three most prominent chocolate manufacturers – Joseph Fry, John Cadbury and Henry Rowntree – were all Quakers. Being teetotal, the Quakers found much to recommend the non-alcoholic beverages of tea, coffee and chocolate.

At the turn of the century when doctors were extremely expensive, the Cadbury employees had regular medicals, and uniforms were provided free of charge. The company was sufficiently far-sighted to appreciate the value of exercise, employing for their female workers a lady who was 'trained in Swedish athletics' and taught not only gymnastics but also swimming and 'numerous games'.

In 1879 when constructing a new factory outside Birmingham, George and Richard Cadbury followed the idea of the French chocolatier Jean Menier and built not only a factory but an entire village –

including a cricket green – for their workforce. Thus Bournville, where the present Cadbury factory is still located, was created. This idea was also taken up by Milton Hershey in Pennsylvania, USA, and when he built his chocolate factory he created the model town of Hersheyville.

Philippe Suchard (1797–1884), the Swiss chocolatier, also possessed a reforming spirit. He was one of the first factory owners ever to insure his workers against accident, something which these days must be done by law.

It was due to the campaigning of the English manufacturers, together with their Swiss and German counterparts, that slavery in the cocoa plantations of Portuguese West Africa, where the moratality rate was as high as 10 per cent, was abolished. This, however, was not before *The Standard*, in 1908, had accused George Cadbury of being indifferent to the 'grimed African hands whose toil is so essential to the beneficent and lucrative operations at Bournville'. Cadbury sued for libel, and though he won his case, having proved that it was through threatening to stop purchasing the West African beans that the slave trade had ceased, the strongly Tory jury, who objected to this rather radical Quaker Liberal, offered him only derisory damages of a farthing.

CHOCOLATE FOLKLORE AND RITUAL

Since the cacao bean was such an important commodity, it was the basis of many Central American rituals. Chocolate was the ceremonial drink of both the Aztecs and the Mayans, served not only at feasts but at births, puberty rites, weddings and funerals. Prisoners of the Aztecs were given chocolate to drink, which was thought would turn their hearts into chocolate. Their hearts were then ripped out and presented to Ekchuah, god of the cacao planters, and the other cacao gods.

The planting of the beans was a special ritual, vivid descriptions of which are given by the 19th-century historian H. H. Bancroft: 'Before planting the seed they held a festival in honour of their gods Ekchuah, Chac and Hobnil, who were their patron deities. To solemnise it, they all went to the plantation of one of their number where they sacrificed a dog having a spot on its skin the colour of cacao. They burned incense to their idols after which they gave to each of the officials a branch of the cacao plant.' There was a strong accent on fertility in the planting ritual as Bancroft also wrote: 'The finest grains of the seed were exposed to the moonlight during four nights . . . the tillers of the soil must sleep apart from their wives and concubines for several days in order that on the night before planting they might indulge their passions to the fullest extent; certain persons were even said to have been appointed to perform the sexual act at the very moment when the first seeds were deposited in the ground.'

The Spanish, who were a superstitious race, thought that it was essential to continue at least some of these customs and attributed the initial failure of cacao trees to thrive in Jamaica to the fact that the English did not bother to perform any rites.

CHOCOLATE LEGENDS

* According to Madame de Sevigné (1626–1696), chocolate has some truly amazing powers. In a letter to her daughter she wrote, 'The Marquise de C took too much chocolate being pregnant last year, that she was brought to bed of a little boy who was as black as the devil.'

* It was said that a nobleman of Louis XIII's court had offended the honour of one of the ladies-in-waiting. She was so incensed that she poisoned a cup of chocolate she prepared him and just before he died, he held her in his arms and whispered, 'The chocolate would have been better if you had added a little more sugar; the poison gives it a bitter flavour. Think of this the next time you offer a gentleman chocolate.'

* The Swedish naturalist Carl Linnaeus (1707–1778), who devoted his life to giving Latin and Greek names to every variety of flora and fauna, gave the cacao tree its official name *Theobroma*, Food of the Gods.

CHOCOLATE AS AN APHRODISIAC

Various claims have been made over the centuries about the aphrodisiacal qualities of chocolate. Casanova declared that it was a great deal more invigorating than champagne, Madame du Barry gave it to all her lovers and Montezuma always consumed large quantities of it before visiting his wives.

In the 17th century it was considered such a violent inflamer of passion that it was thought monks should be banned from drinking it and the theologian Johannes Franciscus Rauch wrote in 1624, 'If such an interdiction had existed, the scandal with which that holy order has been branded might have proved groundless.' Nearly a century later, an article in *The Spectator* in May 1712, warned, 'I shall also advise my fair readers to be in a particular manner careful how they meddle with romances, chocolates, novels and the like inflammers, which I look upon as very dangerous . . .'

Whether or not chocolate is an aphrodisiac, is still open to conjecture. What is true is that there is a relationship between chocolate and being in love – or to be more exact, not being in love. Chocolate contains a chemical called phenylethylamine, which is also found in the human brain. This chemical is a natural amphetamine, which is activated when people are in love, causing the feeling of total euphoria. When someone is not in love and is feeling low and depressed, it is common for them to reach for a bar of chocolate to comfort them, which could be the body's natural reaction to replace the missing chemical.

IS CHOCOLATE GOOD FOR YOU?

U nlike tea and coffee, which have almost no nutritive value at all, the cacao bean is highly nutritious, containing 50 per cent fat, 20–25 per cent carbohydrate, 15–20 per cent protein, 1.5 per cent theobromine, 5 per cent water and 3.5 per cent minerals and vitamins including calcium, iron, magnesium, potassium, sodium, phosphorous, Vitamin A, thiamine, riboflavin and niacin.

At the end of the last century physicians were comparing its properties to those of mother's milk, one writing that 'Cocoa is of domestic drinks the most alimentary; it is without exception the cheapest food that we can conceive, as it may be literally termed meat and drink and were our half-starved artisans and over-worked factory children induced to drink it, instead of the in-nutritious beverage called tea, its nutritive qualities would soon develop themselves in their improved looks and more robust condition.' In a paper read to the Surgical Society of Ireland in 1877, one of its Fellows, Mr Fausett, said, 'I beg respectfully to commend cocoa as an article of infant's food, to the notice of my professional brethen, especially those who, holding office under the Poor Laws, have such large and extensive opportunities of testing its value.'

Today, when the emphasis is on low-fat and low-sugar products, chocolate tends to be regarded as deliciously sinful. The cacao bean itself, however, is a complete food, although nutritionists point out that the fat is saturated. More sinful than the chocolate is the sugar that is added to it, as even bitter chocolate contains two-fifths sugar.

Its value though as a source of quick energy has long been known, Cortés himself commenting, 'One cup of this precious drink allows a man to walk a whole day without taking nourishment.' In 1830 the British navy consumed more cocoa than the rest of the nation together, as it was handed out daily, whilst in the army it was served twice or three times a week. The tradition of its use in the services was continued during the last war when the US government asked Hersheys to develop a high-energy chocolate bar for use by the troops.

However, it was not only the physicians who advocated cocao as being beneficial to health. The French gastronome Brillat Savarin (1775–1826) in his *Physiologie du Gout* remarked, 'The persons who habitually take chocolate are those who enjoy the most equable and constant health and are least liable to a multitude of illnesses which spoil the enjoyment of life.'

There is little documentation about the relationship between cacao and longevity, but a book published in 1903 states 'That it is as nutritious for old as well as young we have interesting proof in the fact that the first Englishman born in Jamaica, Colonel Montague James, who lived to the age of 104, took scarcely any food but cocoa and chocolate for the last thirty years of his life.'

Various medicinal qualities were ascribed to it by the Aztecs, who believed that cacao beans ground with the bones of their ancestors was a cure for diarrhoea, and in the 17th century Spanish women living in Mexico thought that when ground to a paste and mixed with chilli it was 'good for the stomacke, and against the catarre'.

But perhaps one of the most unusual medical uses of chocolate was as a cure for a hangover. On the night of the Coronation of Charles II, Samuel Pepys was excessively drunk and the following day he recorded in his diary: 'Waked in the morning with my head in a sad taking through last night's drink, which I am very sorry for. So rise and went out with Mr Creed to drink our morning draught, which he did give me in chocolate to settle my stomach.'

Although the chocolate contains a very small amount of caffeine, the principal stimulant in it is theobromine, which does not have such a strong effect on the central nervous system as caffeine. It is therefore capable of giving you a 'lift' without any of the toxic effects which are sometimes associated with caffeine. There are some people, however, who find it triggers off headaches and migraines, and it is not recommended for hyperactive children.

'What use are cartridges in battle? I always carry chocolate instead.'
G. B. Shaw (1856–1950), *Arms and the Man*

COCOA BUTTER IN MEDICINE AND COSMETICS

C ocoa butter has an unusual property, in that unlike most vegetable and seed oils (and indeed animal fats) it is solid at room temperature but melts at body heat. This gives it a number of unique pharmaceutical uses. Active ingredients can be added to the basic butter, which is previously deodorised under vacuum; it is, for example, the base most commonly used for contraceptive pessaries.

The cosmetics industry also finds this 'melting property' extremely valuable. Cocoa butter is an excellent skin emollient, being both water insoluble and repellant. When mixed with other ingredients, it is possible to produce a cream which in the jar is quite firm, but when placed on the skin immediately softens and spreads easily and evenly. Cocoa butter therefore forms the base of a large number of moisturisers and after-sun preparations, as well as being added to lipsticks and moisturing lip-balms.

FACTS AND FIGURES

C acao beans are one of the biggest and most important commodities traded in the world markets. On the London futures market alone, from January to December 1985 cocoa trading was worth nearly eighteen thousand million pounds.

West Africa is by far the biggest producer, yielding 1,000,000 tons per annum, followed by Central and South America with 400,000, Asia and Oceana with 55,000 and the West Indies, 45,000. The largest individual producers are Brazil and the Ivory Coast, closely followed by Ghana and Nigeria. For Madagascar, Zaire and Gabon, some of the smaller producers in terms of world trade, cocoa still represents their largest source of income.

The USA is the biggest consumer of cacao beans, although their consumption of approximately 10 lb (4.5 kg) per head per annum is less than half that of Switzerland – a country whose name is almost synonymous with the word chocolate and where they consume 23 lbs (10.4 kg) per year. The UK, however, is not that far behind, with every man, woman and child eating their way through 17 lb (7.7 kg) of chocolate and chocolate confectionery. The West Germans eat a more modest 13½ lbs (6.14 kg) and the French a mere 9 lb (4 kg).

20

FROM CACAO BEANS TO CHOCOLATE

GROWING

Cacao are amongst the most delicate of all tropical trees and will only grow within 20° North and South of the Equator and below 2,500 feet (760 metres). They like a rich, well-drained soil and must be protected from both the wind and intense sunlight. This is achieved by planting larger trees throughout the plantation to shield the cacaos.

In the wild the trees will grow as high as 40–50 feet (12–15 metres), but under cultivation are generally kept to 15–25 feet (4.5–7.5 metres) to facilitate harvesting. The leaves are elongated, glossy and dark green in colour and almost a foot (30 cms) long. The flowers, which are small and pinkish-white, are unusual in that they come out directly from the trunk and larger branches.

From the blossom, about one out of every four or five flowers will successfully mature into pods. The trees produce both blossom and fruit throughout the year, and the pods take approximately five months to ripen, changing from green through to a vivid crimson, before turning a russet brown when they are ready for picking. Each pod, which resembles an elongated furry melon, will contain between 20–50 beans and on average each tree will produce about five pounds (2.25 kg) of beans a year.

There are three main varieties of *Theobroma cacao* which are grown commercially; criollo, forastero and calabacilla. Forastero account for 80 per cent of the world production and are grown mainly in West Africa and Brazil, whilst criollo, which are thinner skinned and have a superior flavour, come from the older, more traditional cacao producing countries of South and Central America and the West Indies, as well as Sri Lanka. Calabacilla, or little pumpkin, produce the poorest-quality beans, which are mainly used for pharmaceutical preparations.

HARVESTING

Harvesting only takes place twice a year. The main crop is generally harvested through October, November and December, whilst the second, smaller crop is picked during April and May. In order to protect the blossom, the ripe pods have to be carefully cut off individually. On the trunk and lower branches this is done with a machette, and with a long-hooked knife for the upper ones.

After picking, the pods are smashed open to reveal the red beans lying in a thick white pulp. The pulp is scooped out and piled on to a covering of banana leaves placed on the ground. This is then covered with more banana leaves and the pile is left to ferment for about six days. Fermentation is an important process as during this time the pulp breaks down and the enzymes in the bean and pulp react on the bean, destroying the bitter acid taste and at the same time increasing the fat content.

Following fermentation the beans are dried for 10–20 days in the sun or, if the humidity is great, with hot air driers. Once the beans have dried they are packed in sacks ready for export.

MANUFACTURE

The first stages of manufacture are common to all chocolatiers in that the beans are thoroughly cleaned and then roasted in large rotating drums until they are of an even colour. Generally a mixture of forastero and criollo beans are used, with the ratio of criollo beans increasing with the quality of the end product; there are some high-quality chocolates which are made only with criollo beans.

Following roasting, the beans are lightly crushed and an artificial wind machine blows away or 'winnows' all the dry outer husks and dust. What is left are partially crushed roasted beans known as 'nibs'.

The 'nibs' are then very finely crushed with rollers to form a thick liquid known as 'mass' which is high in cocoa butter. If this is left to solidify it will form bitter, unsweetened cooking chocolate. More usually, some of it is pressed to remove approximately 50 per cent of the cocoa butter, the exact amount depending on the manufacturer. The pressed 'mass' dries to form a hard cake, which is then ground and re-ground into cocoa powder.

It is after the pressing process that the real skill of the chocolatiers comes to the force – and they are naturally reluctant to divulge the precise way in which the end product is achieved! However, they all use the same basic methods, adding cocoa butter, extracted during the cocoa-making process, into the liquid 'mass'. The amount varies considerably from country to country, but in order for chocolate to be defined as chocolate, rather than 'chocolate flavoured' or 'chocolate cake covering', the regulations in the UK are that plain chocolate must contain a minimum of 30 per cent cocoa solids, and milk chocolate 20 per cent.

Plain chocolate
When making plain chocolate, the 'mass' and cocoa butter are ground together with sugar by a series of rollers with a crushing and shearing action, with each roller moving faster than the next, which produces a considerable amount of frictional heat. Once the chocolate is sufficiently smooth, it is poured into a conche or drum which gently agitates the chocolate for up to three days and helps to mellow the flavour. The final process is 'tempering', to prevent the fat in the chocolate separating, which would give the

chocolate an unattractive, greyish appearance. It is done by cooling the chocolate slightly, then warming it, without allowing the solidified particles of cocoa butter to melt, but increasing the fluidity of the chocolate so that it can be moulded. The chocolate is then ready, either for making into filled chocolates or into bars.

Milk chocolate

For milk chocolate milk has to be condensed by boiling it with sugar in a vacuum. It is then dried in vacuum ovens to make milk 'crumb', which is added to the 'mass' with the cocoa butter and additional sugar and the process continues in the same way as plain chocolate.

MAKING CHOCOLATES

C hocolates are made commercially in two ways, either by 'enrobing' the centres with melted chocolate, or moulding them. Generally it is the cheaper chocolates which are enrobed, whilst the more expensive are moulded, but this depends largely on the nature of the filling as cream fillings must always be moulded and liqueur chocolates are always enrobed.

When chocolates are enrobed, the firm fillings are made into the desired shape and placed on moving wire grids. A curtain of tempered chocolate pours over them, covering the centres and they move down the production line to be cooled. Once the chocolate has been cooled, distinctive patterns can be piped on the top, or in some cases these are marked on to the chocolate as it is starting to cool. 'Enrobed' chocolates have a more rounded edge to them than moulded ones, so it is not difficult to see how a chocolate has been made.

When chocolates are moulded in a factory, first a small amount of chocolate is poured into the moulds, which are then inverted so that the sides also become evenly coated and the excess chocolate drips out. Once this has hardened, the fillings are poured into the centre and a second layer of melted chocolate is poured over for the base. When set, the chocolates are removed from the mould.

Liqueur chocolates, which have a crisp sugar coating between the liquid liqueur and the chocolate, are made by an interesting process. Wide sheets of starch powder are spread out and small indentations are made in them. A solution of hot sugar syrup and liqueur is poured into these depressions and after 1–2 days a coating of sugar forms, completely enveloping the liqueur. The starch powder is then removed and the centres enrobed with chocolate.

MAKING CHOCOLATES AT HOME

Enrobing your favourite fillings with melted chocolate is the easiest way of making chocolates at home. Prepare the fillings, such as fudge, nougat, fondant, etc. Melt the chocolate (see p. 33). Using a two-pronged fork, a fondue fork perhaps, dip the fillings into the chocolate. Allow the excess chocolate to drip back into the bowl and place the dipped chocolate on a piece of non-stick silicone paper or waxed paper to dry.

KEEPING CHOCOLATE IN THE HOME

So long as it is kept in a cool, dry place, away from sunlight and strong odours, milk chocolate can be stored for up to six months and plain chocolate for a year. The ideal temperature is between 12–18°C. Refrigeration is unnecessary and may even impair the flavour slightly. Despite 'tempering', chocolate may develop a slightly chalky bloom which should not affect the flavour to any great extent, and there is certainly nothing to worry about from a health angle.

EASTER EGGS

The word Easter comes from the Old English Eostre, the Teutonic goddess of Spring. Throughout the pagan world, eggs always symbolised the arrival of Spring. The embryonic Christian Church took the Spring festival and made it into its own so that, with the passage of time, eggs came to symbolise the Resurrection. Having become a religious symbol, the eggs were painted and adorned in a variety of ways and by the 17th and 18th century there were eggs encrusted with jewels as well as egg-shaped toys for children.

Making chocolate into eggs for Easter is thought to have started in France in the early part of the 19th century. They would at that time, however, have been very hard and gritty although intricately decorated, as it was not until Joseph Fry had perfected the art of adding cocoa butter to the cocoa 'mass' that it was possible to make moulded chocolates. The Frys produced the first Easter eggs in England in 1873, followed by the Cadburys in 1875, and by

Easter 1893 Cadbury were offering no less than 19 different lines. Easter eggs in England were influenced by those produced in France, Holland and Germany, and it was from Germany that the 'crocodile' finish, which is still used extensively today, came into being. By breaking up the completely smooth surface of the egg, minor imperfections can be disguised.

In addition to eggs, various other simple forms of moulded chocolate started to be made on the Continent in the early part of the 19th century, and this delightful Swiss poem dates from about 1840.

> Jacob, with pistol in his hand,
> exclaims, 'Susannah, dear,
> without your love I'll kill myself!'
> Susannah quakes in fear.
> He lays the pistol to his head,
> Susannah pleads, 'Wait, wait!'
> 'Don't fret,' says Jacob, 'for this gun
> is only chocolate!'

MAKING YOUR OWN EASTER EGGS

It is not difficult to make your own Easter eggs if you have the necessary moulds. The main problem is that having melted down the chocolate (see p. 33), it is difficult to 'temper' it yourself, so that within even a few days the cocoa butter can start to separate out and the eggs take on an unattractive grey colour.

The secret is not to make them too soon before Easter. Before starting to make the eggs, it is important that the moulds are very clean, and it is best to polish the inside of them carefully with kitchen paper.

If children are making the eggs, it is generally better to use chocolate cake covering. Not only is it considerably cheaper, it is also more liquid when warm so that it is easier to work with. If you want to use a premium-quality chocolate, it is worth adding about ½ oz (10 g) of pure white vegetable fat to every 4 oz (110 g) of chocolate, as again this makes the chocolate more liquid and easier to use, whilst not impairing the flavour to any great extent.

Spoon some of the chocolate into the mould and tilt it so that the chocolate evenly coats the inside of the mould. Invert the mould on to a piece of waxed or non-stick silicone paper and leave in a cool place (not the refrigerator) until the chocolate has completely set.

At this stage, you can add a second layer of chocolate which, while not essential, will facilitate removing the chocolate from the mould.

When the chocolate is completely hard and has shrunk away slightly from the edge, gently ease it out with a palette knife. The halves of the egg can then be filled with chocolates or sweets of your choice and the two halves joined together by brushing the rims with a little melted chocolate.

If the egg should crack when you take it out of the mould, don't worry! Simply melt it down and start again.

USING CHOCOLATE FOR COOKING

P *lain and Bitter-Sweet Chocolate* are the most common forms of chocolate used for cooking. The difference between the two is in the proportion of cocoa solids to sugar; generally as the proportion of cocoa solids increases, the proportion of sugar decreases, so that you have a less sweet (i.e. more bitter) chocolate with a stronger flavour for cooking. Plain chocolates start with a minimum of 30 per cent cocoa solids, but some of the Continental chocolates, specifically designed for cooking, have as much as 52 per cent. By law the percentage of cocoa solids must be printed on the pack, so if you check this you can find out if what you are buying is effectively plain or bitter-sweet chocolate.

Milk Chocolate is rarely used in cooking as it does not have a sufficiently concentrated flavour. It is used for making chocolate cases, Easter eggs, chocolates and for decoration.

White Chocolate is made from cocoa butter, flavoured with sugar and vanilla essence. It is not really suitable for cooking as it does not have a true chocolate flavour, although it is occasionally used for mousses.

Cooking or Baker's Chocolate, so called because the first person to produce it was Dr James Baker in the USA and not because it had anything to do with baking, although that is what it tends to be used for. It is unsweetened chocolate, made simply from the roasted bean, without the addition of extra cocoa butter (although some varieties do have small quantities added). Whilst readily available in the USA, it is not easy to find in the UK because it is extremely expensive.

Chocolate Cake Covering is also sometimes referred to as cooking chocolate, which is incorrect. It is a cheaper product than pure chocolate, containing less cocoa solids and a high proportion of vegetable oils (predominantly coconut). Whilst not giving a good flavour in recipes such as chocolate mousse, it is considerably easier to handle than pure chocolate, which makes it practical for children to use for Easter eggs, etc, as well as giving a very satisfactory results in some cakes and steamed puddings.

Cocoa Powder, the cheapest form of chocolate flavouring, is excellent for baking, producing a rich flavour without the addition of excess fat and sugar. It is important, though, that the starch in the powder is cooked, which makes it unsuitable for mousses, icings, etc, although a small amount added to melted plain chocolate will render it stronger and slightly more 'bitter'.

Drinking Chocolate is not generally suitable for cooking because it contains large quantities of sugar, vanilla, etc, so that a great deal has to be used in order to produce a chocolate flavour.

The following flavours are often used in cooking to complement the taste of chocolate:
* *Vanilla essence* enhances almost all chocolate dishes.
* *Salt*, especially when cocoa is used, improves the flavour of cakes, biscuits and cooked desserts. Only a pinch is necessary.
* *Coffee* added in large quantities to chocolate is called mocha. A teaspoon of instant coffee granules with 4 oz (110 g) chocolate makes the finished dish slightly more bitter.
* *Orange*, especially the grated rind, gives chocolate a rich, pungent flavour.

MELTING CHOCOLATE

C are must be taken when melting chocolate not to allow it to become too hot, or to allow steam to circulate round it, because instead of having melted chocolate you will end up with a solid mass. The easiest way is to break the chocolate into small pieces and place it in a basin. Stand the basin over a pan of water ensuring that the steam does not escape between the pan and the sides of the basin. Heat the water to simmering point, then remove from the heat and allow the chocolate to melt, stirring frequently; *the water should not be allowed to boil.*

Small quantities of chocolate can be melted by placing it in a heavy-gauge polythene bag, sealing it, and immersing it in a pan of hot water until the chocolate has melted. The end of the bag can then be snipped off with a pair of scissors and the melted chocolate squeezed out.

Melting chocolate in the oven is not very satisfactory as it is only too easy to over-heat the chocolate. It is, however, extremely successful in a microwave. The chocolate should be broken into pieces, put into a basin and placed in the oven on medium power. For 4 oz (110 g) chocolate in a 1 pint (½ litre) basin allow 2 minutes.

Should the chocolate become thick and difficult to work, this can be rectified by adding a little vegetable oil if you wish to use it for mousses or cakes, but if it is for decoration, such as leaves (see p. 36), this method is not practical as the chocolate will never set very hard again.

CHOCOLATE PETIT FOURS

DIPPING CHOCOLATE

In the United States dipping chocolate is readily available, but it is almost impossible to find in the UK, other than from a few companies that specialise in mail order. You can, however, make your own substitute dipping chocolate by using bitter-sweet chocolate with a high proportion of cocoa solids, and then adding 1 oz (25 g) of white vegetable fat to every 6–8 oz (175–225 g) of chocolate. To make it a little sweeter, add a little sifted icing sugar. In addition to home-made chocolates (see p. 27), you can also make some very simple chocolates and petit fours by dipping fruit and nuts into chocolate.

Nuts are rather difficult to hold, but the large ones, such as Brazil nuts, can be held with kitchen tongs, and the smaller ones, like hazelnuts and almonds, with tweezers. Once completely covered, hold them over the bowl and allow the excess chocolate to drip off before placing on a piece of waxed or non-stick silicone paper to dry off.

Fruits, such as strawberries, grapes, cherries, etc, are also excellent dipped into chocolate. If the fruit has a stalk, keep it on to hold it by, otherwise pierce with a cocktail stick. Dip the fruit into the chocolate so that it comes about half-way up the fruit, allow the excess chocolate to drip off, then place on a piece of waxed paper to dry. Owing to the high water content of fruit, these petit fours do not store well and should be eaten within 24 hours.

CHOCOLATE DECORATIONS

C hocolate lends itself to being made into decorations, which give an attractive finish not only to chocolate dishes but to many other gâteaux and desserts as well.

Grated Chocolate: This is the easiest decoration of all; simply grate the chocolate, using a fairly coarse grater, directly on to the item to be decorated.

Chocolate Curls: Run a potato peeler over the back of the thick bar of chocolate, making sure that the chocolate is not too cold or the curls will break, or too warm when the curls will not hold their shape.

Chocolate Leaves: Any fresh, non-poisonous leaves with well-defined veins can be used to give the shape; rose leaves are ideal. Wash and dry the leaves thoroughly. Dip the underside of the leaf in melted chocolate (see p. 35), then place on a piece of non-stick silicone paper. Leave until the chocolate has hardened, then peel off the leaves and discard.

Chocolate Caraque: This is the professional version of the chocolate curl. Melt the chocolate (see p. 33), then spread with a palette knife on to a working surface so that it is about ¼ inch (½ cm) thick. Leave to harden, then, holding the blade of a knife at an angle of 45°, push away from you and scrape off the long curls. Handle them carefully because they are very fragile and break easily.

CHOCOLATE DRINKS

HOT DRINKS

Hot chocolate, served in big bowls, is still the most common breakfast drink for children in most Continental countries, whilst in the UK it is more often served as a nightcap. Drinking chocolate is the quickest and easiest method of preparing hot chocolate but cocoa has the advantage that it contains less fat and you can sweeten it to taste. As well as serving it plain, there are a number of ways in which hot chocolate can be varied very simply:

SPICY CHOCOLATE: Make the chocolate in the usual way, but when heating the milk add ¼ teaspoon ground cinnamon and a pinch of grated nutmeg and/or allspice for every cup.

CREAMY CHOCOLATE: Just before serving, top each cupful of chocolate with a spoonful of whipped cream and sprinkle with a little drinking chocolate, sieved cocoa, cinnamon or nutmeg.

RUM TODDY: Perfect to warm you up on a cold day and especially popular with skiers. Make up the chocolate as usual, then stir in a measure of dark rum. Top with cream, if wished.

HAPPY MARRIAGE: A great favourite throughout Germany and Switzerland. Use equal parts of hot strong black coffee and hot chocolate, fortified with a little rum or brandy if you feel the need.

HOT CHOCOLATE DE-LUXE: Instead of using cocoa or drinking chocolate, make the hot chocolate using 1 oz (25 g) of good-quality plain or bitter-sweet chocolate for every cup of hot milk. Stir with a cinnamon stick until the chocolate has dissolved, then pour into a cup, add the cinnamon stick and serve topped with a little sieved cocoa.

SPANISH DRINKING CHOCOLATE: Make as above and once the chocolate has melted, remove from the heat and whisk in a raw egg yolk.

COLD DRINKS

For a large proportion of the population, a chocolate milk shake is the ultimate milk shake.

ICE CREAM MILK SHAKE: For each serving, briefly whizz 3 tablespoons of vanilla ice cream, ¼ pint (150 ml) milk and 2 tablespoons of drinking chocolate in a blender or food processor, or use good-flavoured chocolate ice cream and the milk. Sprinkle some drinking chocolate over the surface before serving.

DRINKING CHOCOLATE MILK SHAKE: Blend 2 tablespoons of drinking chocolate together with ¼ pint (150 ml) cold milk and some crushed ice. Pour into a tall glass and serve.

In addition to milk shakes there are some more sophisticated cold chocolate drinks, all of which will serve 4 people.

CAR COCKTAIL: Put 3 oz (75 g) plain chocolate, broken into small pieces into a pan with 1 pint (570 ml) milk. Put over a gentle heat and whisk well until the chocolate has melted. Remove from the heat, allow to cool, then chill. Whisk in ½ pint (275 ml) fresh orange juice, divide between 4 tall glasses and pop a couple of ice cubes into each one. Top each glass with a good swirl of whipped cream, sprinkle with a little drinking chocolate and serve at once with straws.

ICED RUM AND CHOCOLATE: Melt the chocolate in the milk as above and chill, then whisk in 4–5 tablespoons rum and serve in glasses with crushed ice.

MONTEZUMA COCKTAIL: A refreshing, but highly potent, chocolate cocktail recommended by Lindt Chocolates. Melt the chocolate in the milk as above, together with a good pinch of ginger and allspice, and then chill. When cold, add a tablespoon of honey, the grated rind of half a lemon, 4 tablespoons rum and 2 tablespoons of eau de vie. Mix well in a cocktail shaker and serve.

CHOCOLATE LIQUEURS

There are two kinds of Crème de Cacao, a liqueur made from distilling cocoa beans. One is clear and colourless; the other dark brown and slightly sweeter. Although they can be drunk on their own, they are even better made into cocktails.

BRANDY ALEXANDER: Mix equal parts of brandy, crème de cacao and cream together in a cocktail shaker with some crushed ice, then pour into a glass and serve.

GRASSHOPPER: Perfect for chocolate peppermint cream lovers. Mix equal parts of crème de menthe, crème de cacao and cream, then pour over 4–5 ice cubes in a glass and serve.

PUSHKIN: Mix equal parts of gin, vodka and crème de cacao in a cocktail shaker, pour over crushed ice and serve.

Crème de Cacao has other delicious uses:
* Pour it over chocolate, vanilla or coffee ice cream.
* Serve it with orange or strawberry sorbet.
* Add it to chocolate sauces, mousses or pancake fillings.
* Mix it into the icing and filling for sophisticated chocolate cakes.

CHOCOLATE RECIPES

MOLE POBLANO DE GUAJOLOTE (TURKEY IN CHILLI AND CHOCOLATE SAUCE)

One of Mexico's best known national dishes, served on feast days and national holidays. A true *mole*, or chilli sauce, should be made with at least three different varieties of chilli, each giving its own pungent flavour. But for simplicity I have kept to just one. This is a fairly mild version, so if you wish to make it hotter you can increase the quantities of chillies.

7 lb (3 kg) turkey, jointed
1 medium onion, peeled and chopped
2 cloves garlic, crushed
water
2 teaspoons salt
1 teaspoon black peppercorns

Sauce:
6 tablespoons oil
4 green chillies, de-seeded and chopped
2 cloves garlic, crushed
2 onions, peeled and chopped
1/2 teaspoon each cumin seeds and ground allspice
1 teaspoon each coriander seeds and ground cinnamon
6 cloves
2 oz (50 g) blanched almonds
3 tablespoons sesame seeds
1 lb (450 g) tomatoes, roughly chopped
2 oz (50 g) tortilla chips
1 1/2 oz (40 g) bitter-sweet chocolate
salt and freshly milled black pepper

Garnish:
1 tablespoon toasted sesame seeds

Put the turkey pieces into a saucepan with the onion
and garlic. Cover with cold water and add the salt
and peppercorns. Cover and bring to the boil, then
simmer gently for 1 hour or until just tender.
Remove the turkey from the stock and allow to cool,
then take the meat off the bone, discarding the skin,
and cut into 1 inch pieces.

Heat half the oil for a sauce in a large pan and gently fry the chillies, garlic and onions for 5 minutes. Add all the remaining ingredients with the exception of the tortilla chips, chocolate and seasoning, together with 1 pint of the turkey stock. Cover and simmer gently for 25 minutes, stirring from time to time. Crumble in the tortilla chips and cook gently for a further 5 minutes.

Purée the sauce in a blender or food processor, then stir in the chocolate and allow it to melt. Heat the remaining oil in a large pan and quickly fry the turkey pieces for about 5 minutes, then pour over the sauce. Cook gently for a further 10 minutes, stirring frequently. Taste and adjust the seasoning, then turn into the serving dish and sprinkle with the toasted sesame seeds.

Serve with boiled rice, tortilla chips, re-fried beans and guacamole sauce.

Serves 8

43

PIGEONS IN CHOCOLATE SAUCE

It is not surprising that the other nation which uses chocolate extensively in savoury dishes is that of Mexico's conquerors – Spain. Various game hare, pheasant, partridge and pigeon are all cooked with chocolate to form a rich, brown sauce.

4 plump pigeons
1 pint (570 ml) red wine
½ teaspoon freshly ground pepper
1 teaspoon salt
2 cloves garlic, crushed
1 teaspoon dried rosemary
½ teaspoon dried thyme
4 tablespoons olive oil
4 medium-sized onions, peeled and quartered
1 large red pepper, cored and sliced
1 oz (25 g) ground almonds
1 oz (25 g) plain chocolate, broken into small pieces

Place the pigeons in a deep dish. Blend the wine with the pepper, salt, garlic, rosemary and thyme. Pour over the pigeons and leave to marinate for 12–24 hours, turning the pigeons several times.

Heat the oil in a fireproof casserole and gently fry the onions and pepper for 10 minutes. Remove from the pan with a draining spoon and place on one side.

Remove the pigeons from the marinade. Increase the heat under the casserole and quickly fry the pigeons in the remaining oil, until they are lightly browned. Remove from the heat and scatter the onions and pepper over the pigeons. Pour over the marinade. Cover and cook in a very moderate oven, 325°F/160°C/Gas Mark 3 for 2 hours.

Remove from the oven and place the pigeons with the onions and peppers in a heated serving dish, and keep warm. Remove any excess fat from the surface of the liquor and bring to the boil on the top of the cooker. Add the ground almonds and the chocolate and stir until the chocolate has completely melted, then taste and adjust the seasoning and pour the sauce over the pigeons.

Serves 4

RICH CHOCOLATE SAUCE

¼ pint (150 ml) double cream
3 oz (75 g) plain chocolate, broken into small pieces

Put the cream and the chocolate into a small saucepan and heat gently, stirring until all the chocolate has melted and the sauce is piping hot. Pour over profiteroles, ice cream or hot chocolate pudding.

Variations:
* Add 1 teaspoon instant coffee granules for a mocha sauce.
* Add 1–2 tablespoons brandy, rum, or liqueur such as Grand Marnier.
* Add a few drops of peppermint essence for a chocolate peppermint sauce.

Dark Rich Chocolate Cake

2½ oz (60 g) self-raising flour
½ oz (10 g) cocoa powder
4 oz (110 g) plain chocolate, broken into small pieces
3 tablespoons water
4 oz (110 g) butter
4 oz (110 g) caster sugar
4 eggs, separated

Filling:
3 oz (75 g) butter
5 oz (150 g) icing sugar
2 tablespoons strong coffee

Icing:
4 oz (110 g) chocolate, plain, broken into small pieces
4 fl oz (110 ml) double cream
1 tablespoon rum

Grease and line an 8 inch (20 cm) cake tin. Sift together the flour and cocoa. Put the chocolate into a basin with the water and melt (see p. 33). Cream the butter and sugar until light and fluffy, then beat in the egg yolks one at a time. Fold in the flour alternately with the melted chocolate. Whisk the egg whites until they form stiff peaks, then stir in a third of it. Fold in the remainder gently and turn the mixture into the prepared tin.

Bake in a moderate oven 350°F/180°C/Gas Mark 4 for 40–50 minutes or until the top of the cake springs back when lightly pressed. Allow to cool in the tin for a couple of minutes, then turn out on to a wire rack to cool.

Cream the butter for the filling with the icing sugar until light and fluffy, then gradually beat in the coffee. Split the cake into three rounds, divide the filling between the two bottom rounds and re-assemble the cake. Place it on a wire rack with a plate underneath.

Put the chocolate for the icing into a small pan with the cream. Heat gently, stirring frequently, until the chocolate has melted, then remove from the heat and beat in the rum. Allow to cool for 2–3 minutes, until the icing thickly coats the back of the wooden spoon. Using a palette knife, first spread a little of the icing round the sides of the cake, then pour it over the top, allowing the icing to flow evenly down the sides. Leave for about 5 minutes and, when the icing is just beginning to set, make a criss-cross pattern on the top of the cake with a knife.

DEVIL'S FOOD CAKE

One of America's most popular cakes, so-called because, although very light in texture, the cake itself is almost jet black.

6 oz (175 g) flour
1/4 teaspoon baking powder
1 teaspoon bicarbonate of soda
2 oz (50 g) cocoa powder
7 1/2 fl oz (225 ml) water
4 oz (110 g) butter
10 oz (275 g) caster sugar
2 eggs, lightly beaten

Filling:
1 1/2 oz (40 g) butter
2 oz (50 g) icing sugar, sieved
1 1/2 oz (40 g) plain chocolate
1 teaspoon water

Frosting:
2 egg whites
12 oz (350 g) icing sugar, sieved
a pinch of salt and a pinch of cream of tartar
4 tablespoons water

Grease two 8 inch (20 cm) sandwich tins and line the bases with greased greaseproof paper. Sift the flour, baking powder and bicarbonate of soda together. Blend the cocoa with the water.

Cream the butter, add the sugar and beat until light and fluffy. Gradually beat in the eggs a little at a time. Fold in the flour alternately with the cocoa mixture. Divide between the prepared tins and bake in a moderate oven 350°F/180°C/Gas Mark 4 for 45–50 minutes or until just firm to the touch. Leave in the tins for 2 minutes then turn out and cool on a wire rack.

Cream the butter and beat in the icing sugar. Melt the chocolate with the water in a basin (see p. 33). Beat into the butter and sugar and use the filling to sandwich the cakes together.

Put the egg whites, sugar, salt, cream of tartar and water into a large bowl. Place over a pan of hot water and whisk with a hand whisk or an electric beater for about 7 minutes, until the mixture is thick enough to form peaks. Spread over the top and sides of the cake, forming into swirls with a knife and leave to set.

Brillat-Savarin's (1755–1826) recipe for increasing the flavour of chocolate, told to him by the Mother Superior of the Convent of the Visitation, Belley: 'When you want to taste good chocolate, make it the night before in a faience coffee pot and leave it. The chocolate becomes concentrated during the night and this gives it a much better consistency. The good God cannot possibly take offence at this little refinement, since He Himself is everything that is most perfect.'

BROWNIES

The secret of a good Brownie is that it should be moist so care should be taken not to over-cook it. Most Americans claim that it cannot be made with anything other than Baker's chocolate but this version using cocoa gives an excellent result.

2 eggs
8 oz (225 g) caster sugar
2 oz (50 g) butter, melted
1/2 teaspoon vanilla essence
2 oz (50 g) plain flour
3 tablespoons cocoa powder
1/2 teaspoon baking powder
a pinch of salt
2 oz (50 g) walnuts, roughly chopped

Well grease an 8 inch (20 cm) square cake tin. Whisk the eggs and sugar together until the mixture is thick and creamy. Beat in the butter and vanilla essence. Sift in the flour, cocoa, baking powder and salt and fold into the mixture with the walnuts. Turn into the prepared tin and bake in a moderately hot oven, 375°F/190°C/Gas Mark 5, for 30 minutes. Leave in the tin for 10 minutes, then cut the brownies into squares and remove while still warm.

DOUBLE CHOCOLATE CHIP COOKIES

Far superior to the Maryland cookies you can buy in the shops!

1 oz (25 g) cocoa powder
a pinch of salt
6 oz (175 g) self-raising wholemeal flour
3 oz (75 g) light molasses sugar
4 oz (110 g) butter, cut into pieces
2 tablespoons milk blended with ½ teaspoon vanilla
*   essence*
4 oz (110 g) chocolate chips

Sift the cocoa and salt into the mixing bowl. Add the flour and sugar and mix lightly. Rub the butter into the flour until the mixture resembles coarse breadcrumbs. Add the milk to the mixture and mix with your hands to form a firm dough. Dust a working surface *very lightly* with flour and roll out the dough to ¼ inch (½ cm) thickness. Cut out circles approximately 4 inches (10 cm) in diameter and place well apart on greased baking trays to allow for spreading. Sprinkle evenly all over with the chocolate chips, and bake in a very moderate oven 325°F/160°C/Gas Mark 3 for about 15 minutes or until just cooked. Remove from the oven and cool on wire racks.

Makes about 9

CHOCOLATE AND ALMOND STEAMED PUDDING

A deliciously light steamed pudding which can be served either with whipped cream or with the Rich Chocolate Sauce on p. 45.

4 oz (110 g) butter
4 oz (110 g) caster sugar
1/2 teaspoon vanilla essence
4 oz (110 g) plain chocolate cake covering
2 eggs, beaten
2 oz (50 g) self-raising flour
4 oz (110 g) fresh white breadcrumbs
1 oz (25 g) flaked almonds

Butter a 2 pint (1 litre) pudding basin and line the base with a circle of buttered greaseproof paper. Cream the butter with the sugar and vanilla essence until light and fluffy. Melt the chocolate (see p. 33) and allow to cool slightly, then beat into the mixture slowly. Gradually beat in the eggs a little at a time. Sift in the flour and fold in, then fold in the breadcrumbs and almonds. Turn into the prepared basin and cover with a layer of greaseproof paper and foil. Steam for 1½ hours, then invert on to a serving dish and remove the basin.

Serves 4–6

STRAWBERRY FLAN

This makes a very attractive, and impressive summer flan which is quick to prepare. Adding oil to the chocolate not only makes it easier to use but means that when you cut into it the chocolate is a little softer, so does not fly across the room!

6 oz (175 g) milk chocolate
2 tablespoons sunflower oil
1/4 pint (150 ml) double cream
2 tablespoons single cream
8 oz (225 g) strawberries
4 tablespoons strawberry jam
2 tablespoons white wine

Melt the chocolate with the oil (see p. 33), then spread evenly all over the base and sides of an 8¾ inch (22 cm) diameter foil pie plate. Leave to set in a cool place until hard, then very gently and carefully loosen the edges of the foil and peel back the foil plate. Place the chocolate case on a serving dish. Whip the double and single cream together until it holds its shape and spread it over the base of the chocolate. Cut the strawberries in half and arrange them on top. Spoon the jam into a basin, then stir in the wine and spoon over the strawberries to make a glaze.

Serves 4–6

CHOCOLATE ROULADE

It is impossible to make a roulade that does not crack so do not despair if this happens. You can disguise the cracks either with piped cream, or by sprinkling with a little icing sugar.

Cake:
4 eggs, separated
5 oz (150 g) caster sugar
¼ teaspoon vanilla or rum essence
1½ oz (40 g) cocoa powder
icing sugar

Filling:
4 oz (110 g) plain or bitter-sweet chocolate
2 tablespoons rum or water
½ pint (275 ml) double cream, lightly whipped

Decoration:
Chocolate caraque or leaves

Grease a 13 × 9 inch (32.5 × 22.5 cm) swiss roll tin and line with greaseproof or non-stick silicone paper. Whisk the egg yolks, sugar and vanilla or rum essence until thick and creamy. Sift the cocoa powder into the egg yolks and fold in. Whisk the egg whites until they form stiff peaks. Stir 1 tablespoon into the yolks, then fold in the remainder.

Turn the mixture into the prepared tin and spread evenly. Bake in a moderate oven 350°F/180°C/Gas Mark 4 for 15 minutes or until just cooked. Do not over-cook or the roll will crack more easily. Remove from the oven, cover with a clean tea-towel and leave until quite cold. Invert on to a piece of greaseproof or non-stick silicone paper dredged with icing sugar and peel off the baking paper carefully.

Melt the chocolate with the rum or water (see p. 33), and spread evenly over the roulade, then spread three-quarters of the cream over the top. Using the greaseproof or non-stick paper to help you, carefully roll up the roulade and place on a serving dish. Pipe the remainder of the cream along the top and decorate with chocolate caraque or leaves.

Serves 6–8

CHOCOLATE AND PEPPERMINT ICE CREAM

The crunchy pieces of crystallised, peppermint-flavoured sugar in this ice cream give it an unusual texture.

Ice cream:
4 egg yolks
3 oz (75 g) caster sugar
1 pint (570 ml) single cream
3 oz (75 g) plain chocolate, broken into pieces

55

Crystallised peppermint:
4 tablespoons granulated sugar
4 tablespoons water
2 teaspoons peppermint essence

Whisk together the egg yolks and caster sugar until thick and creamy. Put the single cream into a large heavy pan and bring to just above blood heat. Pour over the egg yolks and sugar, whisking all the time. Pour back into the pan and over a *very gentle heat*, continue to cook until the custard coats the back of a wooden spoon. Take care, however, not to allow the custard to curdle. Remove from the heat and add the chocolate, stirring until it has melted, then whisk hard to make sure it is well incorporated.

Pour into a bowl suitable for freezing and allow to cool, then place in the freezer and freeze for about 1½ hours, removing it from the freezer two or three times and beating it hard with a wooden spoon.

Whilst the ice cream is freezing, put the granulated sugar and water into a small, heavy-based pan over a low heat, stirring frequently until the sugar has dissolved. Increase the heat and boil rapidly to 280°F/140°C, or until a small amount of it poured into cold water forms a strand which will crack. Remove quickly from the heat, before it caramelises, and stir in the peppermint essence. Pour quickly on to a piece of non-stick silicone paper and leave until it has become quite cold. Fold over the piece of paper and crush the crystallised sugar with a rolling pin, until it is the texture of coarse breadcrumbs.

Beat the sugar crumbs into the half-frozen ice cream, then return to the freezer and freeze for a further 4 hours or until quite firm. Remove from the freezer, place in the refrigerator for 30 minutes to soften slightly then pile into scoops in individual dishes.

Serves 6

CHOCOLATE MOUSSE

Despite being one of the simplest and most basic chocolate mousses, this is undoubtedly one of the best and can be varied in a number of ways. The recipe below serves four, but an easy way to increase the quantity is to allow 1 egg and 1 oz (25 g) chocolate per person.

4 oz (110 g) plain chocolate broken into pieces
½ oz (10 g) butter
4 eggs, separated

Melt the chocolate with the butter in a large basin (see p. 33). Remove from the heat and beat in the egg yolks, one at a time. Whisk the egg whites until they form stiff peaks, then fold into the chocolate mixture. Turn into 1 large, or 4 small serving dishes, and chill for at least 30 minutes before serving.

Serves 4

Chocolate Mousse Variations:
* Add 2 teaspoons cocoa powder to the chocolate, together with an additional ½ oz (10 g) butter for a more bitter flavour.
* Add 2 teaspoons instant coffee for a mocha flavour.
* Add 1–2 tablespoons dark rum.
* Add the grated rind of an orange, with 1–2 tablespoons Grand Marnier if wished.
* Fold in ¼ pint (150 ml) lightly whipped double cream for a lighter mousse.

CHOCOLATE MARQUISE

One of the richest of all chocolate mousses, but positively ambrosial. This recipe serves eight.

30 sponge finger biscuits
4 tablespoons strong black coffee
6 oz (175 g) plain or bitter sweet chocolate, broken into pieces
4 oz (110 g) unsalted butter
1½ oz (40 g) cocoa powder, sieved
3 egg yolks
4 oz (110 g) caster sugar
¼ pint (150 ml) double cream
¼ pint (150 ml) single cream

Dip each sponge finger quickly into the coffee and use them to line the base and sides of a 2 lb (1 kg) loaf tin, trimming the biscuits to size and placing them sugar side down.

Melt the chocolate (see p. 33) and allow it to cool slightly. Cream the butter, then beat in half the sieved cocoa powder. Beat in the melted chocolate, followed by the remaining cocoa. Whisk the egg yolks with the caster sugar until thick and creamy and fold into the chocolate butter. Whip the double and single cream together until it holds its shape, then fold into the mixture. Turn into the prepared loaf tin, spread it evenly, and chill for at least 1 hour before serving. Turn out on to a serving dish and serve cut in thin slices.

CREAM AND RUM TRUFFLES

These delectable truffles are simply perfect for serving after dinner with coffee, but as they contain fresh cream, they can only be kept for a couple of days and must be stored in the fridge.

5 oz (150 g) plain or bitter sweet chocolate, broken into
pieces
¼ pint (150 ml) double cream
2 egg yolks
2 tablespoons rum
about 2 tablespoons cocoa powder

Put the chocolate into a small pan with the cream. Heat gently, stirring frequently until the chocolate has melted and the mixture is thick. Beat in the egg yolks, one at a time, over a very gentle heat, taking care not to allow the mixture to boil or the yolks will curdle. Remove from the heat and beat in the rum.

Allow to cool slightly, then put into the refrigerator to chill for about 2 hours or until the mixture is very thick. Take teaspoonfuls of the mixture, and roll lightly in your hands to form small balls, then roll these in cocoa powder and place in sweet cases.

Makes about 15

ACKNOWLEDGEMENTS

The author and publishers would like to acknowledge the help of the following:

Cadbury Typhoo Ltd
Chesebrough-Ponds Ltd
The Cocoa, Chocolate and Confectionery Alliance
Lindt & Sprungli Ltd
Rowntree Mackintosh PLC
Joseph Terry & Sons Ltd
J. W. Thornton Ltd

60